Practical
Desserts

p^3

This is a P³ Book
First published in 2003

P³
Queen Street House
4 Queen Street
Bath BA1 1HE, UK

ISBN: 1-40540-921-5

Printed in China

NOTE

This book uses metric and imperial measurements. Follow the same units
of measurement throughout; do not mix metric and imperial.
All spoon measurements are level: teaspoons are assumed to be 5 ml, and
tablespoons are assumed to be 15 ml. Unless otherwise stated,
milk is assumed to be full fat, eggs and individual fruits such as pineapples
are medium.

The nutritional information provided for each recipe is per serving or per person.
Optional ingredients, variations, or serving suggestions have
not been included in the calculations. The times given for each recipe are an approximate
guide only because the preparation times may differ according to the techniques used by
different people and the cooking times may vary as a result of the type of oven used.

Recipes using raw or very lightly cooked eggs should be
avoided by children, the elderly, pregnant women, convalescents,
and anyone suffering from an illness.

Contents

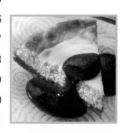

Introduction

For anyone with a sweet tooth, no meal is complete without a sumptuous dessert to finish it off. Desserts come in a multitude of forms, and everyone has their favourite – whether it be the taste of Italy in a tiramisu, a taste of Asia in an exotic fruit salad, or the taste of Britain in a traditional apple pie. All tastes have been catered for in this book.

A historical role

Desserts have enjoyed pride of place on the table through history, around the world. From rich chocolate desserts, which followed the arrival and widespread use of the cocoa bean in western Europe in the eighteenth century, to beautifully simple yet delicious fruit salads made from the fresh fruit of local trees, a dessert is always something special. Desserts have always held an individual place in a meal: they signify a luxury – even in the richest of households. Traditionally the dessert arrives at the end of the meal when people can barely eat any more, yet most manage to eat their share of the pièce de résistance, which may be served with much pomp and ceremony. Ornate dishes, decorative tableware, and the best cutlery are frequently reserved for serving this part of the meal. A successful dessert makes its creator proud and delights everyone.

Spoil yourself

Desserts are a real opportunity to spoil the gourmand in you. You can impress family and friends, make tempting treats for special occasions, birthdays or dinner parties – or simply spoil yourself. With very little effort you can create stunning masterpieces that enhance your table as well as providing a delicious end to a meal.

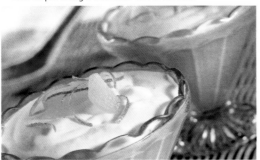

Healthy eating

For those who crave a warm winter dessert or a summer trifle without piling on the calories, recipes have been found that the health-conscious can enjoy. Fruit is an excellent ingredient for low-fat desserts because it is fat-free and naturally sweet. The huge variety of fruit available in supermarkets and greengrocers means that many different flavours and textures can be achieved.

Vegetarian desserts

Vegetarians can enjoy a wealth of dishes from the dessert menu, although strict vegetarians should avoid puddings that contain gelatine. From rich syrup sponges and fruity brûlées, to bread and butter pudding and delicious pancakes, these delicious creations will have all the vegetarians in your household clamouring for more.

Family favourites

This book contains selections of all of your favourite desserts, from sweet rice puddings and delicious apple pies, to irresistible trifles and mouthwatering chocolate biscuits. A sumptuous treat can be found for any time of day or year. Everyone in your household will love the desserts featured within these pages. Some are ideal for parties, while others will be enjoyed after meals or in lunch boxes. Among these irresistible desserts are some new adaptations of old teatime favourites.

Cooking times and techniques

Some desserts may take a while to prepare, others may need to spend time in the oven to cook, and others

will need to be left to cool or stand before serving. Make sure you read the recipe through when planning your meal. Despite the fact that the dessert is probably the last dish to arrive on your table, it may be best to prepare it or begin cooking it first. And remember, all ovens do vary, so alter suggested cooking times in accordance with your oven and keep checking the progress of the dessert when possible.

The following terms are common in dessert recipes and these definitions will help you achieve the best results.

Blending This involves the mixing together of two or more ingredients with a spoon, beater or electric blender until they are completely combined.

Folding This is used to carefully combine light, airy ingredients (such as egg whites) with heavier mixtures (such as cream) without losing too much of the air contained in the lighter one. Folding is a delicate technique where the lighter mixture is placed on top of the heavier one in a bowl sufficiently large to incorporate all the ingredients, with enough room to mix. A rubber spatula is often used to fold ingredients and the mixing should be done slowly and carefully. Cutting down through the mixture from the back of the bowl towards the front and lifting the bottom mixture over the top, whilst turning the bowl a quarter turn after each stroke, is the best method of folding ingredients together. Continue until the two different mixtures are fully combined.

Creaming This method is used to combine ingredients until they are smooth and 'creamy' in texture. Sugar and butter are two ingredients that are frequently combined in this way. The ingredients are creamed when you can no longer see the different constituents and they have formed a homogeneous paste; electric mixers can greatly speed up this process.

Greasing This is essential in baking to stop ingredients sticking to their containers during cooking. Butter is ideal for greasing cake tins or baking sheets. Use greaseproof paper or butter wrappers covered in fat to rub the bottom and sides of the tin or sheet, leaving a thin coating of grease. If asked to grease and flour the container, apply the grease and then sprinkle flour over the top. Shake the container to ensure a complete and even covering and then tip the pan or sheet upside down over the sink to remove any excess flour.

Beating This is the most common way to mix ingredients. Beating means combining all the ingredients using a spoon, fork, or mixer by stirring rapidly in a circular motion. Electric mixers save a lot of time and energy and are better than beating ingredients by hand.

How to make the best desserts
- Start by reading the recipe all the way through.
- Weigh all the ingredients accurately and do basic preparation, such as grating and chopping, before you start cooking.
- Basic cake-making ingredients should be kept at room temperature.
- Mixtures that are creamed should be almost white and have a 'soft dropping' consistency. This can be done by hand, but using a hand-held electric mixer will save time.
- Do not remove a cake from the oven until it is fully cooked. To test if a cake is cooked, press the surface lightly with your fingertips – it should feel springy to the touch. Alternatively, insert a fine metal skewer into the centre of the cake – it will come out clean if the cake is cooked through.
- Leave cakes in their tins to cool before carefully turning out on to a wire rack to cool completely.

KEY	
	Simplicity level 1–3 (1 easiest, 3 slightly harder)
	Preparation time
	Cooking time

Honeyed Rice Puddings

These small rice puddings are quite sweet, but have a wonderful flavour because of the combination of ginger, honey and cinnamon.

NUTRITIONAL INFORMATION

Calories 199	Sugars 15g	
Protein 3g	Fat 1g	
Carbohydrate ...46g	Saturates 0g	

🍚 10 mins   🕐 50 mins

SERVES 4

I N G R E D I E N T S

300 g/10½ oz pudding rice

2 tbsp clear honey, plus extra
  for drizzling

large pinch of ground cinnamon

1 tbsp butter, for greasing

15 no-need-to-soak dried apricots, chopped

3 pieces stem ginger, drained and chopped

8 whole no-need-to-soak dried apricots,
  to decorate

1 Put the rice in a saucepan and just cover with cold water. Bring to the boil, lower the heat, cover the pan, and cook for about 15 minutes or until the water has been absorbed. Stir the honey and cinnamon into the rice.

2 Grease four 150-ml/5-fl oz ramekin dishes with butter.

3 Blend the chopped dried apricots and ginger in a food processor to make a smooth paste.

4 Divide the paste into 4 equal portions and shape each into a flat circle to fit into the bottom of the ramekin dishes.

5 Divide half of the rice among the ramekin dishes and place the apricot paste on top.

6 Cover the apricot paste with the remaining rice. Cover the ramekins with greaseproof paper and foil and steam for 30 minutes or until set.

7 Remove the ramekins from the steamer and leave to stand for 5 minutes.

8 Turn the puddings out on to warm serving plates and drizzle with honey. Decorate with dried apricots and serve.

COOK'S TIP

The puddings may be left to chill in their ramekin dishes in the refrigerator, then turned out and served with ice cream or cream.

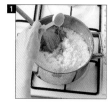

Fruity Queen of Puddings

This is a delicious version of a classic British dessert, made here with fresh bananas and apricot jam.

NUTRITIONAL INFORMATION

Calories	406	Sugars	.......60g
Protein	........13g	Fat	..........7g
Carbohydrate	...77g	Saturates	.......3g

 30 mins   🕐 1 hr

SERVES 4

INGREDIENTS

115 g/4 oz fresh white breadcrumbs

600 ml/1 pint milk

3 eggs

½ tsp vanilla extract

4 tbsp caster sugar

2 bananas

1 tbsp lemon juice

3 tbsp apricot jam

1 Sprinkle the breadcrumbs evenly into a 1-litre/1¾-pint casserole. Heat the milk until just lukewarm, then pour it over the breadcrumbs.

2 Separate 2 of the eggs and beat the yolks with the remaining whole egg. Add to the casserole with the vanilla extract and half the sugar, stirring well to mix. Set aside for 10 minutes.

3 Bake in a preheated oven, 180°C/ 350°F/Gas Mark 4, for 40 minutes until set. Remove the dish from the oven.

4 Slice the bananas and sprinkle with the lemon juice. Spoon the apricot jam on to the pudding and spread out to cover the surface. Arrange the banana slices on top of the apricot jam.

5 Whisk the egg whites until stiff, then add the remaining sugar. Continue whisking until the meringue mixture is very stiff and glossy.

6 Pile the meringue mixture on top of the pudding, return to the oven, and cook for a further 10–15 minutes until the meringue is just set and golden brown. Serve immediately.

COOK'S TIP
This meringue will have a soft texture, unlike a hard meringue, which is cooked slowly for 2–3 hours until dry. Always use a grease-free bowl and whisk for beating egg whites.

Quick Syrup Sponge

You won't believe your eyes when you see just how quickly this light-as-air sponge cooks in the microwave oven!

NUTRITIONAL INFORMATION	
Calories 650	Sugars 60g
Protein 10g	Fat 31g
Carbohydrate . . .89g	Saturates 7g

 15 mins   🕐 5 mins

SERVES 4

I N G R E D I E N T S

140 g/5 oz butter or margarine

4 tbsp golden syrup

6 tbsp caster sugar

2 eggs

125 g/4½ oz self-raising flour

1 tsp baking powder

about 2 tbsp warm water

custard, to serve

1 Grease a 1.5-litre/2¾-pint heatproof basin with a small amount of the butter or margarine. Spoon the syrup into the basin.

2 Cream the remaining butter or margarine with the sugar until light and fluffy. Gradually add the eggs, beating well after each addition.

3 Sift the flour and baking powder together, then fold into the creamed mixture using a large metal spoon. Add enough water to give a soft, dropping consistency. Spoon into the heatproof basin and level the surface.

4 Cover the basin with microwave-proof clingfilm, leaving a small space to let air escape. Microwave on High power for 4 minutes, then remove the sponge from the microwave oven and leave to stand for 5 minutes, while it continues to cook.

5 Turn the sponge out on to a warm serving plate. Serve with custard.

COOK'S TIP

If you do not have a microwave oven, the sponge can be steamed. Cover the basin with a piece of pleated baking paper and a piece of pleated foil. Place the basin in a saucepan, add boiling water, and steam for 1½ hours.

Mixed Fruit Crumble

In this crumble, tropical fruits are flavoured with ginger and coconut, for something a little different and very tasty.

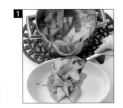

NUTRITIONAL INFORMATION	
Calories 602	Sugars 51g
Protein 6g	Fat 29g
Carbohydrate . . .84g	Saturates 11g

10 mins   50 mins

SERVES 4

I N G R E D I E N T S

2 mangoes, sliced

1 papaya, deseeded and sliced

225 g/8 oz fresh pineapple, cubed

1½ tsp ground ginger

100 g/3½ oz margarine

100 g/3½ oz light brown sugar

175 g/6 oz plain flour

55 g/2 oz desiccated coconut, plus extra
  to decorate

1 Put the sliced mangoes and papaya in a saucepan with the cubed pineapple, ½ teaspoon of the ginger, 2 tablespoons of the margarine and 4 tablespoons of the sugar. Cook over a low heat for 10 minutes until the fruit softens. Spoon the fruit into the bottom of a shallow ovenproof dish.

2 Combine the flour and remaining ginger, then rub in the remaining margarine until the mixture resembles fine breadcrumbs. Stir in the remaining sugar and the coconut and spoon over the fruit to cover completely.

3 Cook in a preheated oven, 180°C/ 350°F/Gas Mark 4, for 40 minutes or until the top is crisp. Decorate with a sprinkling of desiccated coconut and then serve immediately.

Bread & Butter Pudding

Everyone has their own favourite recipe for this dish. This one has added marmalade and grated apples for a really rich and unique taste.

NUTRITIONAL INFORMATION	
Calories 427	Sugars 63g
Protein 9g	Fat 13g
Carbohydrate ...74g	Saturates 7g

 45 mins 1 hr

SERVES 6

I N G R E D I E N T S

4 tbsp butter, softened

4–5 slices white or wholemeal bread

4 tbsp chunky orange marmalade

grated zest of 1 lemon

85–125 g/3–4½ oz sultanas

40 g/1½ oz crystallised mixed peel, chopped

1 tsp ground cinnamon or mixed spice

1 Bramley apple, peeled, cored, and coarsely grated

85 g/3 oz light brown sugar

3 eggs

500 ml/18 fl oz milk

2 tbsp Demerara sugar

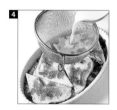

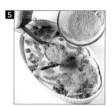

1 Use the softened butter to grease an ovenproof dish and to spread on the slices of bread, then spread the bread with the marmalade.

2 Place a layer of bread in the bottom of the dish and sprinkle with the lemon zest, half the sultanas, half the crystallised peel, half the cinnamon or mixed spice, all of the apple and half the light brown sugar. Add another layer of bread, cutting it so that it fits the dish.

3 Sprinkle over most of the remaining sultanas and all the remaining crystallised peel, with all the remaining spice and light brown sugar, scattering them evenly over the bread. Top with a final layer of bread, again cutting to fit the dish.

4 Lightly beat together the eggs and milk and then carefully strain the mixture over the bread in the dish. If you have enough time, leave the pudding to stand for 20–30 minutes.

5 Sprinkle the Demerara sugar over the top and scatter over the remaining sultanas. Cook in a preheated oven, 200°C/400°F/Gas Mark 6, for 50–60 minutes until risen and golden brown. Serve immediately or leave to cool and serve cold.

Spiced Steamed Pudding

Steamed puddings are irresistible on a winter day, but the texture of this pudding is so light it can be served throughout the year.

NUTRITIONAL INFORMATION

Calories 488   Sugars 56g
Protein . . . . .5g   Fat 19g
Carbohydrate . . .78g   Saturates 4g

15 mins   1½ hrs

SERVES 6

I N G R E D I E N T S

140 g/5 oz butter or margarine, plus extra
  for greasing

2 tbsp golden syrup, plus extra to serve

125 g/4½ oz caster or light brown sugar

2 eggs

175 g/6 oz self-raising flour

¾ tsp ground cinnamon or mixed spice

grated zest of 1 orange

1 tbsp orange juice

90 g/3¼ oz sultanas

2 pieces stem ginger, finely chopped

1 dessert apple, peeled, cored, and
  coarsely grated

1 Thoroughly grease an 850-ml/1½-pint heatproof basin. Put the golden syrup into the basin.

2 Cream the butter or margarine with the sugar until very light and fluffy and pale in colour. Beat in the eggs, one at a time, following each with a spoonful of the flour.

3 Sift the remaining flour with the cinnamon or mixed spice and fold into the mixture, followed by the orange zest and juice. Fold in the sultanas, then the ginger and apple.

4 Turn the mixture into the heatproof basin and level the top. Cover the basin with a piece of pleated, greased baking paper, tucking the edges under the rim of the basin.

5 Cover with a sheet of pleated foil. Tie securely in place with string, with a piece of string tied over the top of the bowl for a handle to make it easy to lift out of the saucepan.

6 Transfer to a saucepan half-filled with boiling water, cover, and steam for 1½ hours, adding more boiling water to the pan as necessary during cooking.

7 To serve the spiced steamed pudding, remove the foil and the baking paper, turn the pudding out on to a warmed serving plate, and serve at once in slices with a little of the golden syrup poured over the top.

Fruity Pancake Bundles

This unusual pancake is filled with a sweet cream flavoured with ginger, nuts and apricots and served with a raspberry and orange sauce.

NUTRITIONAL INFORMATION

Calories 610   Sugars 60g
Protein . . . . .19g   Fat 20g
Carbohydrate . . .94g   Saturates 5g

🧁 15 mins   🕐 35 mins

SERVES 2

I N G R E D I E N T S

B A T T E R

55 g/2 oz plain flour

pinch of salt

¼ tsp ground cinnamon

1 egg

135 ml/4½ fl oz milk

white vegetable fat, for cooking

F I L L I N G

1½ tsp plain flour, sifted

1½ tsp cornflour

1 tbsp caster sugar

1 egg

150 ml/5 fl oz milk

4 tbsp chopped nuts

40 g/1½ oz ready-to-eat dried apricots, chopped

1 piece of stem or crystallised ginger, finely chopped

S A U C E

3 tbsp raspberry jam

4½ tsp orange juice

finely grated zest of ¼ orange

1 To make the batter, sift the flour, salt and cinnamon into a bowl and make a well in the centre. Add the egg and milk and gradually beat in until smooth.

2 Melt a little fat in a medium frying pan. Pour in half the batter. Cook for 2 minutes until golden, then turn and cook the other side for about 1 minute until browned. Set aside and make a second pancake.

3 For the filling, beat the flour with the cornflour, sugar and egg. Gently heat the milk in a pan, then beat 2 tablespoons into the flour mixture. Transfer the flour mixture to the pan and cook gently, stirring constantly, until thick. Remove from the heat, cover with baking paper to prevent a skin forming, and leave to cool.

4 Beat the chopped nuts, apricots and ginger into the cooled mixture, and then put a heaped tablespoonful in the centre of each pancake. Gather and squeeze the edges together to make a bundle. Place in an ovenproof dish and then bake in a preheated oven, 180°C/350°F/Gas Mark 4, for 15–20 minutes until hot and golden but not too brown.

5 To make the sauce, melt the jam gently with the orange juice, then strain. Return to a clean pan with the orange zest and heat through. Serve with the pancakes.

Traditional Apple Pie

This apple pie can be served either hot or cold. The apples can be flavoured with other spices or with grated citrus zest.

NUTRITIONAL INFORMATION

Calories ....577 Sugars 36g
Protein ....6g Fat 28g
Carbohydrate ...80g Saturates 9g

55 mins   50 mins

SERVES 6

INGREDIENTS

800 g–1 kg/1¾–2¼ lb cooking apples, peeled, cored and sliced

125 g/4½ oz brown or white sugar, plus extra for sprinkling

½–1 tsp ground cinnamon, mixed spice or ground ginger

1–2 tbsp water (optional)

SHORTCRUST PASTRY

350 g/12 oz plain flour

pinch of salt

6 tbsp butter or margarine

6 tbsp white vegetable fat

about 6 tbsp cold water

beaten egg or milk, to glaze

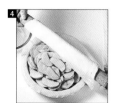

1 To make the pastry, sift the flour and salt into a mixing bowl. Add the butter or margarine with the vegetable fat and rub in with the fingertips until the mixture resembles fine breadcrumbs. Add the water and gather the mixture together into a dough. Wrap the dough in foil and chill for 30 minutes.

2 Roll out almost two-thirds of the dough thinly and use it to line a 20–23-cm/8–9-inch deep pie plate or shallow pie tin.

3 For the filling, mix the apples with the sugar and spice and pack into the pastry case; the filling can come up above the rim. Add the water if needed, particularly if the apples are a dry variety.

4 Roll out the remaining dough to form a lid. Dampen the edges of the pie rim with water and position the lid, pressing the edges firmly together. Trim the edges and crimp them decoratively.

5 Use the leftover trimmings to cut out leaves or other shapes to decorate the pie: dampen them and attach them to the top. Glaze the top of the pie with beaten egg or milk, use a knife to make 1–2 slits in the top, then put the pie on a baking sheet.

6 Bake the pie in a preheated oven, 220°C/425°F/Gas Mark 7, for about 20 minutes, then lower the temperature to 180°C/350°F/Gas Mark 4 and cook for 30 minutes or until the pastry is a light golden brown. Serve the pie hot or cold, sprinkled with brown or white sugar.

Baked Semolina Pudding

Succulent plums simmered in orange juice and spices complement this rich and creamy semolina pudding perfectly.

NUTRITIONAL INFORMATION

Calories	304	Sugars	. . . . .32g
Protein	. . . . .9g	Fat	. . . . .12g
Carbohydrate	. . .43g	Saturates	. . . . . . .4g

🍲 5 mins   🕐 45 mins

SERVES 4

I N G R E D I E N T S

2 tbsp butter or margarine

600 ml/1 pint milk

finely pared rind and juice of 1 orange

55 g/2 oz semolina

pinch of grated nutmeg

2 tbsp caster sugar

1 egg, beaten

TO DECORATE

small knob of butter

grated nutmeg

SPICED PLUMS

225 g/8 oz plums, halved and stoned

150 ml/5 fl oz orange juice

2 tbsp caster sugar

½ tsp mixed spice

1 Grease a 1-litre/1¾-pint ovenproof dish with a little of the butter or margarine. Put the milk, the remaining butter or margarine, and the orange rind in a saucepan. Sprinkle in the semolina and bring to the boil over a low heat, stirring constantly. Simmer gently for 2–3 minutes. Remove the pan from the heat.

2 Add the nutmeg, orange juice and sugar, stirring well. Add the beaten egg and stir to mix.

3 Transfer the mixture to the prepared dish and bake in a preheated oven, 190°C/375°F/Gas Mark 5, for 30 minutes until lightly browned.

4 To make the spiced plums, put the plums, orange juice, sugar and spice into a saucepan and simmer gently for about 10 minutes until the plums are just tender. Remove the pan from the heat and set aside to cool slightly.

5 Top the semolina pudding with a knob of butter and a sprinkling of grated nutmeg, and serve with the spiced plums.

Cherry Clafoutis

This is a hot dessert that is simple and quick to put together. Try the batter with other fruits – apricots and plums are particularly delicious.

NUTRITIONAL INFORMATION

Calories 261	Sugars 24g	
Protein 10g	Fat 6g	
Carbohydrate . . .40g	Saturates 3g	

10 mins   40 mins

SERVES 6

I N G R E D I E N T S

125 g/4½ oz plain flour

4 eggs, lightly beaten

2 tbsp caster sugar

pinch of salt

600 ml/1 pint milk

butter, for greasing

450 g/1 lb stoned black cherries,
    fresh or canned

3 tbsp brandy

1 tbsp sugar, to decorate

3 Thoroughly grease a 1.7-litre/3-pint ovenproof serving dish with butter and pour in about half of the batter.

4 Spoon over the cherries and pour the remaining batter over the top. Sprinkle the brandy over the batter.

5 Bake in a preheated oven, 180°C/ 350°F/Gas Mark 4, for 40 minutes or until risen and golden brown.

6 Remove from the oven and sprinkle over the sugar just before serving. Serve the clafoutis warm.

1 Sift the flour into a large mixing bowl. Make a well in the centre and add the eggs, sugar and salt. Gradually draw in the flour from around the edges and whisk until incorporated.

2 Pour in the milk and whisk the batter thoroughly until very smooth.

Fruit Brûlée

This is a cheat's brûlée, in that yogurt is used to cover a layer of fruit, before being sprinkled with sugar and grilled.

NUTRITIONAL INFORMATION	
Calories 311	Sugars 48g
Protein 7g	Fat 11g
Carbohydrate . . .48g	Saturates 7g

🥧 1¼ hrs   🕐 15 mins

SERVES 4

INGREDIENTS

4 plums, stoned and sliced

2 cooking apples, peeled and sliced

2 tbsp water

1 tsp ground ginger

600 ml/1 pint Greek-style yogurt

2 tbsp icing sugar, sifted

1 tsp almond extract

85 g/3 oz Demerara sugar

1 Put the plums and apples in a saucepan with 2 tablespoons of water and cook for 7–10 minutes until tender but not mushy. Set aside to cool, then stir in the ground ginger.

2 Using a slotted spoon, lift out the fruit and spoon into the bottom of a shallow, heatproof serving dish.

3 Combine the yogurt, icing sugar and almond extract and spoon on to the fruit to cover.

4 Sprinkle the Demerara sugar over the top of the yogurt mixture and cook under a hot grill for 3–4 minutes or until the sugar has melted and formed a crust.

5 Set aside to chill in the refrigerator for 1 hour before serving.

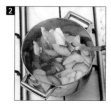

Tropical Salad

In this recipe, ripe tropical fruits are blended with rum and orange juice.
You could serve them in the shells of baby pineapples for a stunning effect.

NUTRITIONAL INFORMATION

Calories	69	Sugars	........13g
Protein	.........1g	Fat	..........0.3g
Carbohydrate	...14g	Saturates	......0g

 10 mins   🕐 0 mins

SERVES 8

I N G R E D I E N T S

1 papaya

2 tbsp fresh orange juice

3 tbsp rum

2 bananas

2 guavas

1 small pineapple or 2 baby pineapples

2 passion fruit

pineapple leaves, to decorate

scooped-out baby pineapple shells,
    to serve (optional)

1 Cut the papaya in half and remove the seeds. Peel and slice the flesh into a bowl.

2 Pour the orange juice over the papaya in the bowl, then pour over the rum.

3 Slice the bananas, peel and slice the guavas, and add them to the bowl.

4 Cut the top and bottom from the pineapple, then cut off the skin.

5 Slice the pineapple flesh, discard the core, cut the flesh into pieces, and add to the bowl.

6 Halve the passion fruit, scoop out the flesh with a teaspoon, add to the bowl, and stir well to mix.

7 Spoon the fruit salad into glass bowls or scooped-out baby pineapple shells. Decorate with pineapple leaves and serve.

COOK'S TIP

Guavas have a heavenly smell when ripe – their scent will fill a whole room. They should yield to gentle pressure when ripe, and their skins should be yellow. The canned varieties are very good and have a pink tinge to the flesh:

Orange Syllabub

This is a zesty, creamy whip made from yogurt and milk with a
hint of orange, served with light and luscious sweet sponge cakes.

NUTRITIONAL INFORMATION	
Calories 464	Sugars 74g
Protein 22g	Fat 5g
Carbohydrate . . .89g	Saturates 2g

1½ hrs   10 mins

SERVES 4

I N G R E D I E N T S

4 oranges

600 ml/1 pint low-fat natural yogurt

6 tbsp skimmed milk powder

4 tbsp caster sugar

1 tbsp grated orange zest

4 tbsp orange juice

2 egg whites

strips of orange zest, to decorate

S P O N G E   H E A R T S

2 medium eggs

6 tbsp caster sugar

40 g/1½ oz plain flour

40 g/1½ oz wholemeal flour

1 tbsp hot water

1 tsp icing sugar

1 Slice off the tops and bottoms of the
oranges and remove the skin. Then
cut out the segments, removing the zest
and membranes between each one. Divide
the orange segments between 4 dessert
glasses, then chill.

2 In a mixing bowl, combine the yogurt,
milk powder, sugar, orange zest, and
orange juice. Cover and chill for 1 hour.
Whisk the egg whites until stiff, then fold

into the yogurt mixture. Spoon on to the
orange slices and chill for an hour.
Decorate with strips of orange zest.

3 To make the sponge hearts, line a
15 x 25-cm/6 x 10-inch baking tin
with baking paper. Whisk the eggs and
caster sugar together until thick and pale.
Sift the flours, then fold into the eggs,
using a large metal spoon, adding the hot
water at the same time.

4 Pour into the prepared tin and bake in
a preheated oven, 220°C/425°F/Gas
Mark 7, for 9–10 minutes until golden on
top and firm to the touch.

5 Turn the sponge out on to a sheet of
baking paper. Using a 5-cm/2-inch
heart-shaped cutter, stamp out hearts
from the sponge. Transfer to a wire rack to
cool. Lightly dust with icing sugar before
serving with the syllabub.

New Age Spotted Dick

This is a deliciously moist low-fat dessert. The sauce is in the centre of the dessert, and will spill out when the sponge is cut.

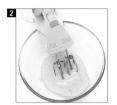

NUTRITIONAL INFORMATION

Calories	529	Sugars	........41g
Protein	.........9g	Fat	..........31g
Carbohydrate	...58g	Saturates	......4g

25 mins   1¼ hrs

SERVES 6–8

I N G R E D I E N T S

125 g/4½ oz raisins

125 ml/4 fl oz water

125 ml/4 fl oz corn oil, plus extra for greasing

125 g/4½ oz caster sugar

25 g/1 oz ground almonds

2 eggs, lightly beaten

175 g/6 oz self-raising flour

S A U C E

60 g/2¼ oz walnuts, chopped

60 g/2¼ oz ground almonds

300 ml/10 fl oz semi-skimmed milk

4 tbsp granulated sugar

1 Put the raisins in a saucepan with the water. Bring to the boil, then remove from the heat. Set aside to allow the raisins to steep for 10 minutes, then drain.

2 Whisk together the oil, sugar and ground almonds until thick and syrupy; this will need about 8 minutes of beating (on medium speed if using an electric whisk).

3 Add the eggs, one at a time, beating well after each addition. Combine the flour and raisins. Stir into the mixture.

4 Brush a 1-litre/1¾-pint heatproof basin with oil, or line with baking paper.

5 To make the sauce, put all the ingredients into a saucepan. Bring to the boil, stir, and simmer for 10 minutes.

6 Transfer the sponge mixture to the greased basin and pour on the hot sauce. Place on a baking sheet.

7 Bake in a preheated oven, 180°C/350°F/Gas Mark 4, for about 1 hour or until well risen. Lay a piece of baking paper across the top of the sponge if it starts to brown too quickly.

8 Leave to cool for 2–3 minutes in the basin before turning out on to a warm serving plate.

COOK'S TIP

Always soak raisins before baking them because they retain their moisture nicely and you can taste their full flavour instead of biting on a dried-out raisin.

Mascarpone Cheesecake

Lemon and ginger give this baked cheesecake a wonderfully tangy flavour. Ricotta cheese could be used as an alternative to mascarpone.

NUTRITIONAL INFORMATION	
Calories 327	Sugars 25g
Protein 9g	Fat 18g
Carbohydrate ...33g	Saturates 11g

 15 mins   50 mins

SERVES 4

I N G R E D I E N T S

1½ tbsp unsalted butter, plus extra
for greasing

150 g/5½ oz ginger biscuits, crushed

25 g/1 oz stem ginger, chopped

500 g/1 lb 2 oz mascarpone cheese

finely grated rind and juice of 2 lemons

100 g/3½ oz caster sugar

2 large eggs, separated

fruit coulis (see Cook's Tip), to serve

1 Grease a 25-cm/10-inch springform cake tin or loose-based tin with butter and line the base with baking paper. Brush the paper with butter.

2 Melt the remaining butter in a pan and stir in the biscuits and ginger. Use the mixture to line the tin, pressing the mixture about 5 mm/¼ inch up the sides.

COOK'S TIP

Make a delicious fruit coulis by cooking 400 g/14 oz fruit, such as blueberries, for 5 minutes with 2 tablespoons of water. Strain, then stir in 1 tablespoon (or more to taste) of sifted icing sugar. Leave to cool before serving.

3 Beat together the cheese, lemon rind and juice, sugar, and egg yolks until quite smooth.

4 Whisk the egg whites until they are stiff, then fold them into the cheese and lemon mixture.

5 Pour the mixture into the prepared tin and bake in a preheated oven, 180°C/

350°F/Gas Mark 4, for 35–45 minutes until it is just set. Do not worry if it cracks or sinks – this is quite normal.

6 Remove the cheesecake from the oven. Leave in the tin to cool completely.

7 Serve the cheesecake with a fruit coulis (see Cook's Tip).

Egg Mousse with Marsala

This warm mousse is known as *zabaglione* in Italy. It will not keep, so make it fresh and serve immediately.

NUTRITIONAL INFORMATION

Calories ....158 Sugars 29g
Protein ....1g Fat 1g
Carbohydrate ...29g Saturates 0.2g

  15 mins   0 mins

SERVES 4

INGREDIENTS

5 egg yolks

100 g/3½ oz caster sugar

150 ml/5 fl oz Marsala wine or sweet sherry

fresh fruit or amaretti biscuits,
   to serve (optional)

1 Place the egg yolks in a heatproof bowl. Add the sugar to the egg yolks and whisk until the mixture is thick and very pale and has doubled in volume.

2 Place the bowl containing the egg mixture over a pan of simmering water.

3 Add the Marsala wine or sherry to the egg mixture and continue whisking until the mixture becomes warm and foamy. This process may take as long as 10 minutes.

4 Pour the mixture, which should now be foamy and light, into 4 wine glasses.

5 Serve the mousse warm with fresh fruit or amaretti biscuits, if you desire.

COOK'S TIP

Any other type of liqueur may be used instead of the Marsala wine or sweet sherry, if you prefer. Serve soft fruits, such as strawberries or raspberries, with the warm mousse – it is a delicious combination.

Quick Tiramisu

This is a quick version of one of the most popular of all Italian desserts. It can be prepared in a matter of minutes.

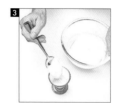

NUTRITIONAL INFORMATION	
Calories 387	Sugars 17g
Protein 9g	Fat 28g
Carbohydrate ...22g	Saturates 15g

 15 mins   0 mins

SERVES 4

I N G R E D I E N T S

225 g/8 oz mascarpone or full-fat cream cheese

1 egg, separated

2 tbsp natural yogurt

2 tbsp caster sugar

2 tbsp dark rum

2 tbsp strong black coffee

8 sponge fingers

2 tbsp grated plain or milk chocolate

1 Put the cheese in a large bowl, add the egg yolk and yogurt, and beat together until smooth.

2 Whisk the egg white until stiff but not dry, then whisk in the sugar and carefully fold into the cheese mixture.

COOK'S TIP

Mascarpone is an Italian soft cream cheese made from cow's milk. It has a rich, silky smooth texture and a deliciously creamy flavour. It can be eaten as it is with fresh fruits or flavoured with coffee or chocolate.

3 Spoon half of the mixture into 4 sundae glasses.

4 Mix together the rum and coffee in a shallow dish. Dip the sponge fingers into the rum mixture, break them in half, or into smaller pieces if necessary, and divide among the glasses.

5 Stir any remaining coffee mixture into the remaining cheese and spoon over the top.

6 Sprinkle. with grated chocolate. Serve immediately or chill until required.

Summer Fruit Dessert

A sweet cream cheese dessert that complements the tartness of fresh summer fruits very well.

NUTRITIONAL INFORMATION

Calories	725	Sugars	........36g
Protein	........10g	Fat	..........59g
Carbohydrate	...36g	Saturates	......36g

5 mins, plus 1 hr 20 mins chilling   0 mins

SERVES 4

INGREDIENTS

450 g/1 lb mascarpone cheese

4 egg yolks

100 g/3½ oz caster sugar

400 g/14 oz frozen summer fruits, such as raspberries and redcurrants

whole redcurrants, to decorate

amaretti biscuits, to serve

1 Place the mascarpone cheese in a large mixing bowl and beat with a wooden spoon until smooth.

2 Stir the egg yolks and sugar into the mascarpone cheese, mixing well. Cover and leave the mixture to chill in the refrigerator for about 1 hour.

3 Spoon a layer of the chilled mixture into the bottom of 4 individual serving dishes. Spoon a layer of the frozen summer fruits on top. Repeat the layers in the same order, reserving some of the mascarpone mixture for the top.

4 Chill the mascarpone mousses in the refrigerator for about 20 minutes. The fruits should still be slightly frozen. Decorate with whole redcurrants and serve with amaretti biscuits.

VARIATION
Try adding 3 tablespoons of your favourite liqueur to the mascarpone cheese mixture in step 1, if you prefer.

Panettone with Strawberries

Panettone is a sweet Italian bread. It is delicious toasted on the barbecue and topped with mascarpone and marinated strawberries.

NUTRITIONAL INFORMATION

Calories 475   Sugars 20g
Protein . . . . .7g   Fat 31g
Carbohydrate . . .36g   Saturates 19g

5 mins, plus
30 mins
chilling

2 mins

SERVES 4

I N G R E D I E N T S

225 g/8 oz strawberries

2 tbsp caster sugar

6 tbsp Marsala wine

½ tsp ground cinnamon

4 slices panettone

4 tbsp mascarpone cheese

1 Hull the strawberries, then slice them from top to bottom and place in a bowl. Add the sugar, Marsala wine and ground cinnamon to the strawberries.

2 Toss the strawberries in the sugar and cinnamon mixture until they are well coated. Leave to chill in the refrigerator for at least 30 minutes.

3 When ready to serve, transfer the slices of panettone to a rack set over medium–hot coals. Cook the panettone for about 1 minute on each side or until golden brown.

4 Remove the toasted panettone from the barbecue and transfer to serving plates. Top with the mascarpone cheese and strawberries, and serve immediately.

Rich Vanilla Ice Cream

Italy is synonymous with ice cream. This home-made version of real vanilla ice cream is absolutely delicious and so easy to make.

NUTRITIONAL INFORMATION

Calories	652	Sugars	.......33g
Protein	.........8g	Fat	..........55g
Carbohydrate	...33g	Saturates	......32g

🍨 5 mins, plus 1 hr cooling ⏱ 10 mins

SERVES 4–6

I N G R E D I E N T S

600 ml/1 pint double cream

1 vanilla pod

pared zest of 1 lemon

4 eggs, beaten

2 egg yolks

175 g/6 oz caster sugar

1 Place the cream in a heavy saucepan and heat gently, whisking. Add the vanilla pod, lemon zest, eggs and egg yolks and heat until the mixture reaches just below boiling point.

2 Lower the heat and cook for 8–10 minutes, whisking the mixture continuously until thickened. Stir the sugar into the cream mixture, set aside, and leave to cool, then strain the cream mixture through a sieve.

3 Slit open the vanilla pod, scoop out the seeds, and stir into the cream.

4 Pour the mixture into a shallow, freezer-proof container with a lid and freeze overnight until set.

COOK'S TIP

For a smoother ice cream, beat the frozen mixture in order to break up the ice crystals, then freeze again. Alternatively, process the mixture in an ice-cream maker.

Mango Mousse

This is a light, softly set, and tangy mousse, which is perfect for clearing the palate after a meal of mixed flavours.

NUTRITIONAL INFORMATION

Calories 346   Sugars 27g
Protein ....7g   Fat 24g
Carbohydrate ...27g   Saturates 15g

⏱ 40 mins   🕐 0 mins

SERVES 4

INGREDIENTS

400 g/14 oz canned mangoes in syrup

2 pieces stem ginger, chopped

200 ml/7 fl oz double cream

4 tsp powdered gelatine

2 tbsp hot water

2 egg whites

1½ tbsp light brown sugar

stem ginger and thin strips of lime zest,
    to decorate

1 Drain the mangoes, reserving the syrup. Blend the mango pieces and ginger in a food processor or blender for 30 seconds, or until smooth.

2 Measure the mango purée and make up to 300 ml/10 fl oz with the reserved mango syrup.

3 In a separate bowl, whip the cream until it forms soft peaks. Fold the mango mixture into the cream until well combined.

4 Dissolve the gelatine in the hot water and leave to cool slightly.

5 Pour the gelatine into the mango mixture in a steady stream, stirring. Cool in the refrigerator for 30 minutes until almost set.

6 Beat the egg whites in a clean bowl until they form soft peaks, then beat in the sugar. Gently fold the egg whites into the mango mixture with a metal spoon.

7 Spoon the mousse into individual serving dishes, decorate with stem ginger and lime zest, and serve.

COOK'S TIP

The gelatine must be stirred into the mango mixture in a gentle, steady stream to prevent it setting in lumps when it comes into contact with the cold mixture.

Exotic Fruit Pancakes

These pancakes are filled with an exotic array of tropical fruits. Decorate them lavishly with edible flowers or mint sprigs.

40 mins   35 mins

SERVES 4

I N G R E D I E N T S

B A T T E R

125 g/4½ oz plain flour

pinch of salt

1 egg

1 egg yolk

300 ml/10 fl oz coconut milk

4 tsp vegetable oil, plus extra for cooking

F I L L I N G

1 banana

1 papaya

juice of 1 lime

2 passion fruit

1 mango, peeled, stoned, and sliced

4 lychees, stoned and halved

1–2 tbsp honey

edible flowers or sprigs of fresh mint, to decorate

1 Sift the flour and salt into a bowl. Make a well in the centre and add the egg, egg yolk and a little of the coconut milk. Gradually draw the flour into the egg mixture, beating well, and gradually adding the remaining coconut milk to make a smooth batter. Stir in the oil. Cover and chill for 30 minutes.

2 Peel and slice the banana and place in a bowl. Peel and slice the papaya, discarding the seeds. Add to the banana with the lime juice and mix well. Cut the passion fruit in half and scoop out the flesh and seeds into the fruit bowl. Add the mango, lychees and honey, and stir in.

3 Heat a little oil in a 15-cm/6-inch frying pan. Pour in just enough of the pancake batter to cover the bottom of the pan and tilt so that it spreads thinly and evenly. Cook until the pancake is just set and the underside is lightly browned, then turn it over and briefly cook the other side. Remove from the pan and keep warm. Repeat with the remaining batter to make a total of 8 pancakes.

4 To serve, place a little of the prepared fruit filling along the centre of each pancake and then roll into a cone shape. Lay the pancakes, seam side down, on warmed serving plates, decorate with edible flowers or mint sprigs, and serve.

Coconut Cream Custards

Smooth, creamy, and refreshing – these tempting little custards are made with an unusual combination of coconut, cream and eggs.

NUTRITIONAL INFORMATION	
Calories 288	Sugar 24g
Protein 4g	Fat 20g
Carbohydrate ...25g	Saturates 14g

10 mins   45 mins

SERVES 8

I N G R E D I E N T S

C A R A M E L

125 g/4½ oz granulated sugar

150 ml/5 fl oz water

C U S T A R D

300 ml/10 fl oz water

90 g/3¼ oz creamed coconut, chopped

2 eggs

2 egg yolks

1½ tbsp caster sugar

300 ml/10 fl oz single cream

T O   S E R V E

sliced banana or slivers of fresh pineapple

1–2 tbsp freshly grated coconut or
desiccated coconut

1 Have ready 8 small ovenproof dishes of about 150-ml/5-fl oz capacity. To make the caramel, place the granulated sugar and water in a saucepan and heat gently to dissolve the sugar, then boil rapidly, without stirring, until the mixture turns a rich golden brown.

2 Immediately remove the pan from the heat and dip the base into a bowl of cold water to prevent the caramel cooking further. Quickly but carefully divide the caramel among the ovenproof dishes to coat the bases.

3 To make the custard, place the water in the same pan as you used for the caramel, add the coconut, and heat, stirring constantly, until the coconut dissolves. Place the eggs, egg yolks, and sugar in a bowl and beat well with a fork. Add the hot coconut milk and stir well to dissolve the sugar. Stir in the cream and strain the mixture into a jug.

4 Arrange the dishes in a roasting tin and fill with enough cold water to come halfway up the sides of the dishes. Pour the custard mixture over the caramel

in the dishes, cover with kitchen foil, and then cook in a preheated oven, 150°C/300°F/Gas Mark 2, for about 40 minutes or until set.

5 Remove the dishes, leave to cool, then chill overnight. To serve, run a knife around the edge of each dish and turn out on to a serving plate.

6 Serve the custards with slices of banana or slivers of fresh pineapple, sprinkled with freshly grated coconut or desiccated coconut.

Banana & Mango Tart

Bananas and mangoes are a great combination of colours and flavours, especially when topped with toasted coconut chips.

NUTRITIONAL INFORMATION

Calories 235	Sugars 17g
Protein 4g	Fat 10g
Carbohydrate . . .35g	Saturates 5g

1¼ hrs   5 mins

SERVES 8

I N G R E D I E N T S

20-cm/8-inch ready-made pastry case

F I L L I N G

2 small ripe bananas

1 mango, sliced

3½ tbsp cornflour

6 tbsp Demerara sugar

300 ml/10 fl oz soya milk

150 ml/5 fl oz coconut milk

1 tsp vanilla extract

toasted coconut chips, to decorate

1 Slice the bananas and arrange half of them in the pastry case with half of the mango pieces.

2 Put the cornflour and sugar in a saucepan and mix together. Gradually whisk in the soya milk and coconut milk until combined. Simmer over a low heat, whisking constantly, for 2–3 minutes until the mixture thickens.

3 Stir in the vanilla extract, then spoon the mixture over the fruit.

4 Top with the remaining fruit and the toasted coconut chips. Chill in the refrigerator for 1 hour before serving.

COOK'S TIP

Coconut chips are available in some supermarkets and most health food shops. They are worth using because they look more attractive and are not so sweet as desiccated coconut.

Almond Trifles

Amaretti biscuits made with ground almonds have a high fat content. If you prefer, use biscuits made from apricot kernels for a lower fat content.

Calories 241	Sugars 23g
Protein 9g	Fat 6g
Carbohydrate . . .35g	Saturates 2g

 1¼ hrs   0 mins

SERVES 4

I N G R E D I E N T S

8 amaretti biscuits

4 tbsp brandy or Amaretto liqueur

225 g/8 oz raspberries

300 ml/10 fl oz low-fat custard

300 ml/10 fl oz low-fat natural fromage frais

1 tsp almond extract

2 tbsp flaked almonds, toasted

1 tsp cocoa powder, for dusting

1 Place the biscuits in a mixing bowl and, using the end of a rolling pin, carefully crush them into small pieces.

2 Divide the crushed biscuits among 4 serving glasses. Sprinkle over the brandy or liqueur and set aside for about 30 minutes to soften.

3 Top with a layer of raspberries, reserving a few for decoration, and spoon over enough custard just to cover.

4 Combine the fromage frais with the almond extract and spoon the mixture over the custard, smoothing the surface. Refrigerate for about 30 minutes.

5 Before serving, sprinkle with the toasted flaked almonds and dust with cocoa powder.

6 Decorate the trifles with the reserved raspberries and serve immediately.

VARIATION
Try this trifle with assorted summer fruits. If they are a frozen mix, use them frozen and let them thaw so that the juices soak into the biscuit layer – it will taste delicious.

Mini Florentines

Serve these biscuits at the end of a meal with coffee, or
arrange in a shallow presentation box for an attractive gift.

NUTRITIONAL INFORMATION

Calories 75   Sugars 6g
Protein ....1g   Fat 5g
Carbohydrate ....6g   Saturates 2g

🍰 🍰 🍰

🧈 30 mins   🕐 10–12 mins

MAKES 40

INGREDIENTS

6 tbsp butter, plus extra for greasing

75 g/2¾ oz caster sugar

2 tbsp sultanas or raisins

2 tbsp chopped glacé cherries

2 tbsp chopped crystallised ginger

25 g/1 oz sunflower seeds

100 g/3½ oz flaked almonds

2 tbsp double cream

175 g/6 oz plain or milk chocolate

1 Grease and flour 2 baking sheets or line with baking paper.

2 Place the remaining butter in a small saucepan and heat gently until melted. Add the sugar, stir until dissolved, then bring the mixture to the boil. Remove from the heat and stir in the sultanas or raisins, cherries, ginger, sunflower seeds and almonds. Mix well, then beat in the cream.

3 Place small teaspoons of the fruit and nut mixture on to the prepared baking sheets, allowing plenty of space for the mixture to spread. Bake in a preheated oven, 180°C/350°F/Gas Mark 4, for 10–12 minutes or until light golden.

4 Remove from the oven and, whilst still hot, use a circular biscuit cutter to pull in the edges to form perfect circles. Leave to cool and go crisp before removing from the baking sheet.

5 Break the chocolate into pieces, place in a heatproof bowl over a saucepan of simmering water, and stir until melted. Spread most of the chocolate on to a sheet of baking paper. When the chocolate is on the point of setting, place the biscuits flat-side down on the chocolate and let it harden completely.

6 Cut around the florentines and remove from the baking paper. Spread a little more melted chocolate on the coated side of the florentines and use a fork to mark waves in the chocolate. Leave to set. Arrange the florentines on a plate (or in a presentation box for a gift) with alternate sides facing upwards. Keep them cool.

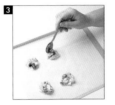

Apple Fritters

These apple fritters are coated in a light, spiced batter and deep-fried until crisp and golden. Serve warm with this unusual almond sauce.

NUTRITIONAL INFORMATION

Calories	438	Sugars	........15g
Protein	.........6g	Fat	..........32g
Carbohydrate	...35g	Saturates	.......4g

🍧 15 mins   🕐 15 mins

SERVES 4

INGREDIENTS

100 g/3½ oz plain flour

pinch of salt

½ tsp ground cinnamon

175 ml/6 fl oz warm water

4 tsp vegetable oil

2 egg whites

2 dessert apples, peeled

vegetable oil or sunflower oil, for deep-frying

caster sugar and cinnamon,
   to decorate

ALMOND SAUCE

150 ml/5 fl oz natural yogurt

½ tsp almond extract

2 tsp clear honey

---

4 Using a sharp knife, cut the apples into chunks and dip the pieces of apple into the batter to coat.

5 Heat the oil for deep-frying to 180°C/350°F, or until a cube of bread browns in 30 seconds. Cook the apple pieces, in batches if necessary, for about 3–4 minutes until they are light golden-brown and puffy.

6 Remove the apple fritters from the oil with a slotted spoon and drain on absorbent kitchen paper.

7 Mix together the caster sugar and the cinnamon and sprinkle over the warm fritters.

8 Mix the sauce ingredients in a serving bowl and serve with the fritters.

1 Sift the flour and salt together into a large mixing bowl.

2 Add the cinnamon and mix well. Stir in the warm water and vegetable oil to make a smooth batter.

3 Whisk the egg whites until stiff peaks form and fold into the batter.

 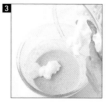 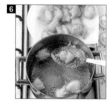